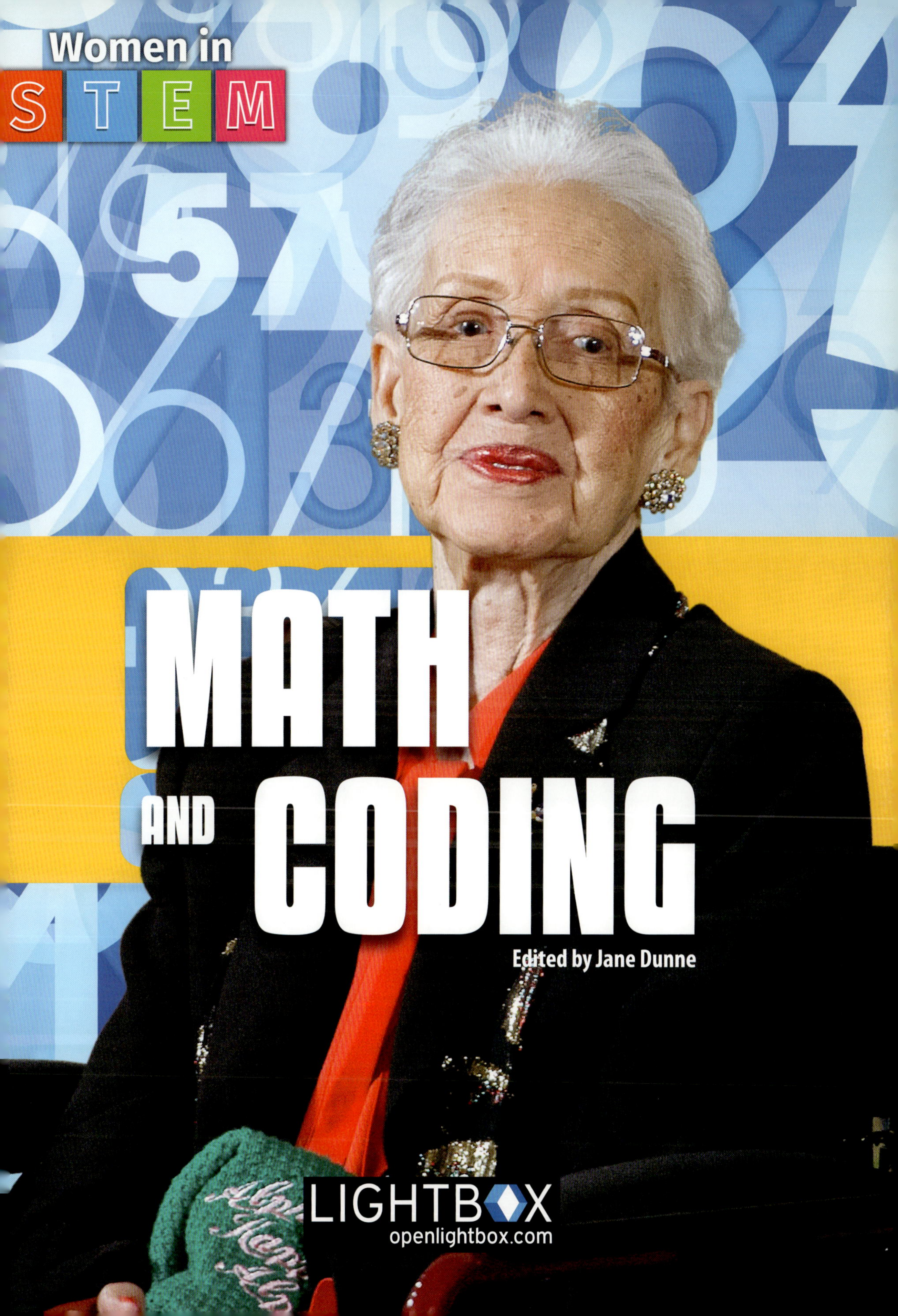

Women in STEM

MATH AND CODING

Edited by Jane Dunne

LIGHTBOX
openlightbox.com

LIGHTBOX

Go to
www.openlightbox.com
and enter this book's
unique code.

ACCESS CODE

LBXX5288

Lightbox is an all-inclusive digital solution for the teaching and learning of curriculum topics in an original, groundbreaking way. Lightbox is based on National Curriculum Standards.

STANDARD FEATURES OF LIGHTBOX

AUDIO High-quality narration using text-to-speech system

ACTIVITIES Printable PDFs that can be emailed and graded

SLIDESHOWS Pictorial overviews of key concepts

VIDEOS Embedded high-definition video clips

WEBLINKS Curated links to external, child-safe resources

TRANSPARENCIES Step-by-step layering of maps, diagrams, charts, and timelines

INTERACTIVE MAPS Interactive maps and aerial satellite imagery

QUIZZES Ten multiple choice questions that are automatically graded and emailed for teacher assessment

KEY WORDS Matching key concepts to their definitions

Women in STEM

MATH AND CODING

CONTENTS

Women in Math and Coding

Most people use math on a daily basis, although they are not always aware of it. Anything to do with numbers, quantities, and shapes involves the use of math. Practical applications for math are usually based on theories.

Computer sciences developed from the possibilities first revealed by mathematical theories. Computer coding instructions are written in mathematical language. Ada Lovelace invented the first **computer program** in the mid-1800s, and women excelled in math whenever they were given the opportunity to study it.

There are many respected women mathematicians, but the number of women taking math courses remains small.

There is evidence from marks carved into bones that early people were counting the days of the month or the number of animals they hunted. From about 3,000 BC, the people of Sumeria and Egypt used counting systems to keep track of animals, foodstuffs, and building materials such as tiles and bricks. There are texts about math dating from 1,900 BC. The ancient Greeks Pythagoras and Euclid produced many of the rules about math that are used today.

In the 300s AD, Hypatia, the first woman mathematician, wrote about shapes, curves, and angles. This branch of math is called **geometry**. In about 830 AD, math took another step forward when it was realized that some problems could be solved using letters in place of numbers. This branch of math is called algebra.

In the United States, about 40 percent of math graduates are women. However, very few of these women go on to further math studies after gaining their degree. This is surprising, because in the field of biology, women are well represented. Why this might be is the subject of considerable research and debate.

WOMEN IN SCIENCE, 1967 TO 2017

Total percentage of all PhDs earned by women, plus percentage earned in biology, and math and statistics

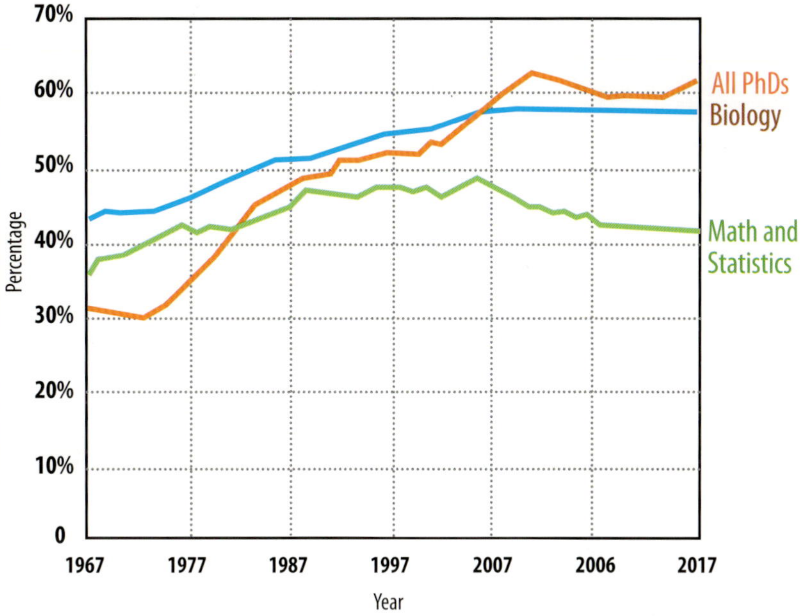

Total percentage of all bachelor degrees earned by women, plus percentage earned in biology, and math and statistics

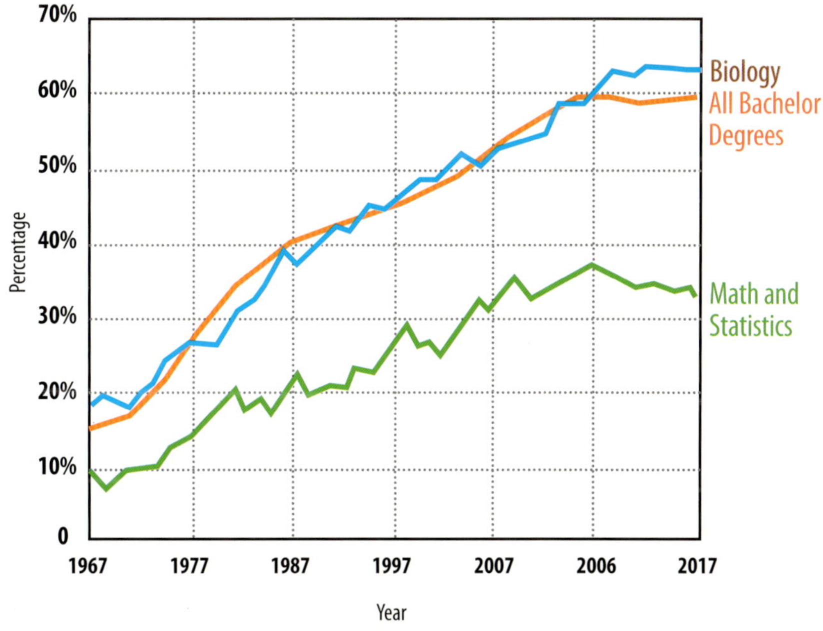

Math and Coding Worldwide

The work of thinkers in the ancient world laid the foundations of math. In about 387 BC, the **philosopher** Plato founded the Academy in Athens. By 600 BC, ancient Greece was the mathematical center of the world. Engineers in the Roman Empire, which was founded in 27 BC, used math calculations for practical activities such as building roads and bridges. However, during the Middle Ages, from 476 AD to 1453 AD, math and science were barely studied in Europe. The Islamic World and India became places of innovation in the subject, building on the theories of the ancient Greeks.

By the 1600s and 1700s, scientists such as Isaac Newton and Gottfried Liebniz were developing mathematical theories in Europe. During this period, women found it difficult to get a good education in math because they were not allowed to attend university. Things began to change in the 1800s. The first American woman to be awarded a PhD in math was Winifred Edgerton Merrill, in 1886.

London, Great Britain
Ada Lovelace was an aristocrat who had been educated in math. In 1833, she was shown an early type of computer by Charles Babbage in London. She immediately realized its possibilities, and wrote the first computer program.

Virginia, United States
Katherine Johnson's math skills played an important role at the **NASA** laboratory in Virginia. She calculated the **flight paths** for crewed space flights.

Arctic Ocean
Göttingen, Germany
While teaching at Germany's University of Göttingen, mathematician Emily Noether developed "Noether's theorem," which solved a problem in modern physics. She also made important innovations in the study of algebra while working at the university.
Seoul, South Korea
In 2014, Iranian mathematician Maryam Mirzakhani received the Fields Medal, the highest award in math, in Seoul for her work on Riemann's Surfaces. These are an important part of modern geometry that involve complex curves.
Atlantic Ocean
EUROPE
ASIA
Pacific Ocean
AFRICA
Indian Ocean
Nanjing, China
In the late 1700s, Wang Zhenyi undertook private studies in math and astronomy in Nanjing. She rewrote Chinese math texts, and explained the work of Pythagoras for Chinese children to understand.
AUSTRALIA
MAP LEGEND
Land
Water
N
SCALE
0
1,000 miles
1,000 kilometers
Southern Ocean
ANTARCTICA

Hypatia of Alexandria

Name: Hypatia
Born: About 350 AD, Alexandria, Egypt
Died: 415 AD, Alexandria, Egypt
Occupation: Mathematician, astronomer
Education: Neoplatonic School of Alexandria. She was given an education in math by her father.
Major discoveries and achievements: Editor of Ptolemy's *Almagest*, and Diophantus' *Arithmetica*

Hypatia was the daughter of a mathematician. Her father was Theon of Alexandria, who was recognized as the Roman Empire's leading math expert at the time. Alexandria was a great center of Greek learning and culture, and Theon's greatest achievement was editing a new edition of *Elements*. This was a book on geometry by the Greek mathematician Euclid, who had been writing in the third century BC.

Little is known about Hypatia's early life, but writers of the time specifically mentioned her as being a great astronomer and mathematician. Hypatia also became a respected teacher of philosophy. Some writers described how she gave lectures in the open air, attracting audiences from all over the world. Hypatia is known to have edited an edition of the *Almagest*, written by Ptolemy, the Alexandrian astronomer and mathematician, in about 150 AD. In the book, Ptolemy had written about the movements of the stars and planets in the universe, with Earth at the center.

Hypatia was admired and respected during her lifetime. Her lectures were well attended.

Hypatia was killed by a mob that pulled her from her chariot. Her murder may have been part of a local political dispute.

Hypatia is thought to have made her own corrections to some of Ptolemy's calculations while she edited the book. Hypatia is also known to have written a commentary on a well-known work by the Greek mathematician Diophantus. The work, in 13-volumes, was called *Arithmetica*. Hypatia was one of Alexandria's first female teachers, and it is thought that she created a version of *Arithmetica* for her students.

As well as her research in mathematical theory, Hypatia was an inventor, too. She appears to have invented a device called an astrolabe, which was used to identify stars and planets, and measure their height above the horizon. The astrolabe later became an important instrument for **navigation** at sea.

Hypatia was a pagan, meaning she worshipped the gods and goddesses of ancient Rome at a time when Christianity had become the religion of the Roman Empire. In Alexandria, the Christian Roman governor respected Hypatia's views. She even became his advisor. However, a new bishop quarreled with the governor. In 415, Hypatia was attacked and killed by a mob of Christians. The event shocked the Roman world. Other pagan philosophers in Alexandria fled to Athens to escape Christian persecution.

GREEK THOUGHT AND ARAB SCHOLARS

The Christians who dominated the final decades of the Roman Empire had little respect for the theories of Greek thinkers. Christians destroyed the famous Greek library at Alexandria in 391. The library had been the largest and most important in the ancient world. Some Greek books survived, however.

In the 700s, Muslim Arab invaders conquered much of the Middle East. They took over cities, such as Alexandria, that had been important centers of Greek learning. They preserved any books they found. Al-Mansur, the caliph or ruler of the Islamic world, set up a huge library to store these texts, and ordered they be translated into Arabic. Islamic scholars then studied these works, and added to the original texts. These Arab collections kept Greek scientific research and learning alive.

Ada Lovelace

Name: Augusta Ada King, Countess of Lovelace
Born: 1815, London, Great Britain
Died: 1852, London, Great Britain
Occupation: Mathematician and computer programmer
Education: Privately educated. The writer Mary Somerville, known as the "queen of science," was among her tutors.
Major discoveries and achievements: Created a computer program to drive the Analytic Engine, an early computer

Ada Lovelace was the daughter of Lord Byron. He was a famous poet in the early nineteenth century. Byron left his wife one month after Ada was born. Ada never saw her father, who died when she was eight years old. Ada's mother was a mathematician. She wanted Ada to have a good education. Most girls from wealthy families were home-schooled at the time, and Ada was taught privately. Her mother hired tutors to teach her many subjects. Ada was educated in math by some of the best mathematicians of the day.

When she was 12 years old, Ada tried to make wings that would allow her to fly. She studied the anatomy of birds, and drew plans for a flying machine. She also wrote a book called *Flyology* to record her experiments. She impressed her tutors. One of them said that Ada could become an important mathematician one day.

Ada said she was a "poetical scientist." She saw no conflict between art and science and believed that imagination was important for scientists.

Charles Babbage's Difference Engine was a large mechanical calculator.

Computer programs perform calculations using only **0 and 1**.

The chess computer **Deep Blue** could look at **200 million chessboard moves** per second.

In 2018, the world's most powerful **supercomputer** was **1,432,513** times faster than the most powerful supercomputer in 1993.

One of Ada's tutors was Mary Somerville, a science writer and mathematician. In 1833, Somerville introduced Ada to Charles Babbage, a math professor. He showed Ada a prototype for what he called a "Difference Engine," a calculating machine. He later proposed a machine that he called the "Analytical Engine."

Even though the Analytical Engine was never completed, Ada was excited by it, and quickly grasped what it might be able to achieve. In 1842, she translated a French article about Babbage's machine. The notes she added to her translation contained a description of how to use the machine to calculate a sequence of numbers that could be used to represent other things. This was the first description of an **algorithm**. Ada recognized that the Analytical Engine could be used to do more than generate numbers. She had realized that this machine could be set up to compose music and play chess, and that increasing the speed of its calculations would lead to even greater possibilities. Today's computers change music, text, pictures, and sounds into digital number patterns, which can then perform new functions.

Ada also used her math skills to try to predict the results of horse races. This idea was a disaster, however, and she abandoned it. Ada was working on the connections between numbers and music when she died. The computer language "Ada" was named for her.

Emmy Noether

Name: Amalie Emmy Noether
Born: 1882, Erlangen, Germany
Died: 1935, Bryn Mawr, Pennsylvania
Occupation: Mathematician, physicist
Education: University of Erlangen
Major discoveries and achievements: The Noether **theorem**
Major honors: Ackermann–Teubner Memorial Award, 1932

Emmy Noether was the daughter of a mathematician. Her father, Max Noether, invented various theorems. Emmy was a good student and studied French, English, and music at school. At the time, women needed these qualifications if they wanted to teach at a girls' school. However, Emmy decided not to become a teacher. Instead, she decided to go to the University of Erlangen. She was one of just two women among 986 students. At university, Emmy realized that math was her preferred subject. She completed her PhD in 1907.

German universities did not admit many women in the early 1900s. At the University of Göttingen, Emmy had to advertise her lectures under the name of the math faculty professor, David Hilbert.

Women were not officially allowed to teach in universities. At the University of Göttingen, Emily worked without pay until 1923. Her family supported her during this period.

Noether taught at the University of Erlangen, and then at the University of Göttingen. While at Göttingen, she produced Noether's theorem. Emmy's theorem described the relationship between energy, time, and **momentum**. In very simple terms, whether a ball is thrown in the air tomorrow or next week, its route through the air will always be the same. Noether's theorem solved some of the problems in Albert Einstein's theory of gravitation, the revolutionary theory of general relativity. Einstein described Emmy as the most significant creative mathematical genius of the time.

The **Nazis** came to power in Germany in 1933. In April, Emmy was removed from her post because she was Jewish. She moved to Bryn Mawr College in Pennsylvania. In 1935, a colleague said Emmy was "the greatest woman mathematician who has ever lived."

THE ROAD TO MODERN MATH

Pythagoras was born in Greece in about 570 BC. He studied math and geometry in Egypt. He and his followers, Pythagoreans, believed that the whole universe could be described by numbers.

Euclid wrote *Elements* in about 300 BC. Over 13 chapters, he set out mathematical theorems, definitions, and **mathematical proofs**. Many of his ideas are used today.

Muhammad ibn Mūsā al-Khwārizmī was a Persian mathematician. His work on algebra is regarded by many as the foundation of the sciences. Algebra is named for his book, *Hisab al-Jab wa-al-Muqabala*, written in about 820 AD.

Gottfried Wilhelm Leibniz and Isaac Newton invented calculus in the mid-1600s. This was a way of making calculations about the behavior of a moving body, such as a planet, or a continuous curve.

Carl Friedrich Gauss was a **polymath**. He is recognized for his groundbreaking work in geometry, astronomy, and number theory. He wrote *Arithmetical Investigations* in 1801, which became a very influential math book.

Grace Hopper

Name: Grace Murray Hopper
Born: 1906, New York City, New York
Died: 1992, Arlington, Virginia
Occupation: Navy admiral, computer scientist
Education: Vassar College, Yale University
Major discoveries and achievements: Programming the Mark I computer, creating computer language COBOL
Major honors: World War II Victory Medal, Defense Distinguished Service Medal, Presidential Medal of Freedom

From an early age, Grace showed an interest in engineering. When she was seven years old, she wanted to know how alarm clocks work, so she took all the clocks in her home apart. After doing well at high school, Grace went on to study math and physics at Vassar College, and received her PhD in math at Yale in 1934. She became a professor at Vassar. When the United States entered World War II, Grace tried to enlist in the U.S. Navy, but was refused on the grounds that her job at Vassar was too important.

Grace and the other women who programmed calculating machines in the 1940s were known as "computers."

However, in 1943, Grace resigned from Vassar and joined the U.S. Naval Reserve. This was a period when the U.S. armed forces were testing computers. The Army was using the Electronic Numerical Integrator and Computer at Pennsylvania University. This computer was largely staffed by women programmers.

For the Navy, Grace worked on the Mark I, a computer set up at Harvard University. The Mark I was one of the first computers to carry out long calculations. Grace was in charge of a team of women who wrote the programs for the machine. Programming the Mark I was labor intensive. Grace encouraged her team to share common parts of their programs to save time. She also wrote the first computer manual. This was a 500-page guide to the Mark I.

Grace stayed at Harvard after the war. In the 1950s, she invented the first compiler, a computer program that used written words, rather than patterns of 0s and 1s. Some scientists thought this was impossible, but Grace's system worked. The compiler made it quicker for programmers to input information. This led to the development of the first universal computer language, COBOL. COBOL stands for Common Business Oriented Language.

Rear Admiral Grace Hopper was the oldest officer still on active duty when she retired on board USS *Constitution* in August 1986.

The **Mark I computer** weighed more than **10,000 pounds** (4,500 kilograms).

The **Mark I computer had** **750,000** electrical components.

A modern **cell phone** just **6 inches** (15 centimeters) long has more computing power than the Mark I.

Grace remained with the U.S. Naval Reserve throughout her career. She became a captain in 1973, a commodore in 1983, and a rear admiral in 1985. Grace was a creative leader of teams. After retirement she was a popular public speaker. Her talks inspired people to think creatively about computer science.

Katherine Johnson

Name: Katherine Coleman Goble Johnson
Born: 1918, White Sulphur Springs, West Virginia
Occupation: Mathematician, physicist
Education: West Virginia State University, West Virginia University
Major discoveries and achievements: Calculating flight paths for first U.S. crewed space flights and for the Apollo moon landing of 1969
Major honors: Presidential Medal of Freedom, 2015

Katherine Johnson was gifted in math from an early age. However, her hometown did not provide any public schooling for African American children after eighth grade. Katherine had to attend West Virginia High School, many miles (km) away from her home. She left high school when she was 14 and enrolled at the West Virginia State College. At the age of 18, Katherine graduated with highest honors in math and French. In 1939, she attended West Virginia University graduate school after a Supreme Court ruling of 1938 ruled that the university could not refuse admission to African Americans.

At NASA, Katherine was promoted and given greater responsibilities when her skills in analytic geometry became known.

In 1952, Katherine heard that the government department for space exploration, which later became NASA, was hiring African American women to work at the Langley laboratory. Katherine started working there in 1953. She was part of an otherwise all-male team calculating flight paths. There were strict rules about **segregation** in Virginia. Katherine found that she had to fight not only racial segregation, but also some of her male supervisors who did not want women at their meetings, or to be named as authors of reports.

Katherine's first big achievement occurred when she planned the flight path for the first American in space. The flight was in 1961. The astronaut was Alan Shepard. Katherine also calculated backup plans.

In the early 1960s, mechanical computers were introduced at NASA. Many people distrusted the new machines. Astronaut John Glenn was due to make the first piloted **orbit** of Earth. He did not believe the computer calculations he was given. He knew the math had to take into account the Moon's **gravitational pull**. Glenn asked Katherine to check the math by hand before he would fly. On February 20, 1962, Glenn successfully orbited the Earth in *Friendship 7*, and returned safely. The mission was a success.

Katherine's work was important to the success of the Apollo space program. She worked on the Apollo 11 moon landing mission in 1969, but perhaps her most important work was for the Apollo 13 mission. The spacecraft launched on April 11, 1970. Shortly afterward, an explosion crippled the craft. Katherine's work on backup procedures and flight paths contributed to the safe return of the spacecraft and its crew on April 17. Katherine said that everybody had been worried about getting Apollo 13 to the Moon, but she had been concerned about getting them back. Katherine worked for NASA for 33 years, before her retirement, contributing to space shuttle missions and plans for the exploration of Mars.

The space shuttle program was just one of the many programs that Katherine worked on during her time with NASA.

Glenn's orbit around the Earth covered **75,679 MILES** (121,794 kilometers).

Friendship 7 **traveled** at about **17,500 miles per hour** (28,200 km/h).

Friendship 7 reached a **height** above Earth of **162 MILES** (261 km).

Maryam Mirzakhani

Name: Maryam Mirzakhani
Born: 1977, Tehran, Iran
Died: 2017, Stanford, California
Occupation: Mathematician
Education: Sharif University of Technology, Harvard University
Major discoveries and achievements: Proof of Shor's Algorithm, showing that complex curves are a regular shape
Major honors: Blumenthal Award, 2009; Fields Medal, 2014

Maryam showed her talents from an early age and attended a special school for gifted children in Tehran. She won gold medals in national math competitions. As a teenager, she became the first Iranian woman to qualify for the annual math competition known as the International Mathematical Olympiad. She scored 41 points out of a possible 42. The next year, she achieved a perfect score.

In her early twenties, Maryam developed a mathematical proof for a process known as Shor's Algorithm. This brought her international recognition. She moved to the United States in 1999, and was awarded her PhD from Harvard in 2004. She became a professor at Stanford University in California in 2009.

Maryam once described her relationship to math. She said it was like being lost in a jungle and then having to find a way out by using all existing knowledge looked at in new ways. Her major work was focussed on the problems of finding the shortest route between two points on certain kinds of curved objects. In particular, she worked on a set of shapes called "Riemann surfaces."

Maryam was presented with the Fields Medal in Seoul, South Korea, in 2014. She was the first woman to win it. The Fields Medal is the leading international prize for young mathematicians.

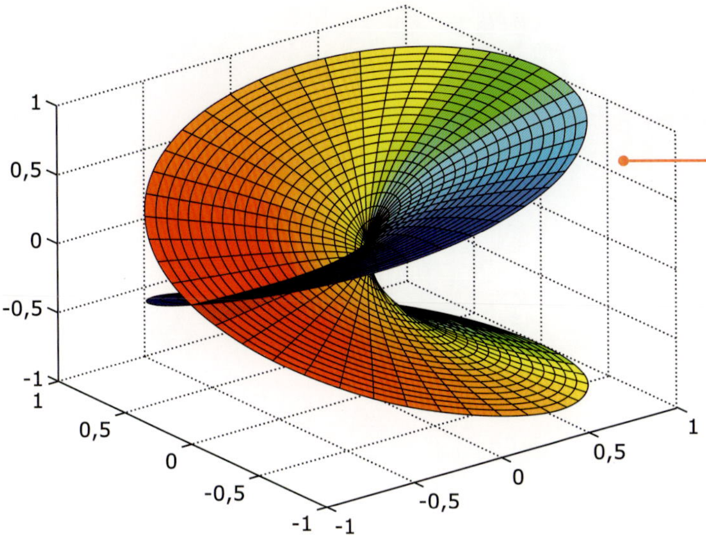

Riemann's surfaces are named after Bernhard Riemann. He was a nineteenth century German mathematician who studied geometry and shapes made by curves.

Maryam's research involved a very complicated process. What she did was described as being like someone studying the movement of the balls on a pool table. However, she not only studied one table, she worked out what could happen on all the possible pool tables in the world.

Then, she worked out what would happen on all possible pool tables if the table itself started to changed shape.

Maryam was diagnosed with cancer in 2016, and died the following year. In her honor, her birthday, May 12, is celebrated as International Women in Mathematics Day.

WINNER OF MATH COMPETITIONS

Maryam was a successful competitor in math competitions. The International Mathematical Olympiad has been held annually since 1959. More than 100 countries send national teams to the Olympiad. In order to qualify for a national team, students have to show outstanding ability in math. There are no team prizes, but awards are presented to the top 50 percent of contestants. All who take part must be under the age of 20, and must not be in education above high-school level. Several youthful participants in the event have gone on to win the Fields Medal. Maryam was one of them.

Canadian Zhuo Qun Song is the most successful IMO contestant. He has five gold medals.

Timeline of Math and Coding

From earliest times, people have counted, calculated, and observed forms and shapes in nature. The work of ancient mathematicians laid the foundations of math, and many of their ideas are still taught today. Most of these early mathematician were men. Women were refused the right to a university education in math until the late 1800s. It is only since than that women mathematicians have made their mark.

1900 BC | 500 AD | 1850 | 1880 | 1900

1900 BC
The first known multiplication tables and geometric exercises are written down by Babylonian scholars in central-southern Mesopotamia, now modern-day Iraq.

415 AD
Hypatia, the leading mathematician of the ancient Roman world, is murdered by a mob in ancient Alexandria.

1843
Ada Lovelace writes what is considered the first real computer program.

1918
Emmy Noether's theorem on energy, time, and momentum is published.

The **abacus** was invented in China. Learning how to use an abacus is a good introduction to math, especially arithmetic.

1950 | 1960 | 2000 | 2010 | 2019

1952
Grace Hopper invents the compiler, allowing computer programmers to input words instead of patterns of numbers.

1961
Katherine Johnson works out the flight path for the U.S. crewed space orbit around Earth.

2019
May 12 is celebrated as the first Women in Mathematics Day, in honor of Maryam Mirzakhani.

1945
Kay McNulty, Betty Jennings, Betty Snyder, Marlyn Meltzer, Fran Bilas, and Ruth Lichterman program the Electronic Numerical Integrator and Computer (ENIAC) at the University of Pennsylvania. This was the first electronic, general-purpose computer.

2008
Barbara Liskov wins the Turing Award for her work in the development of modern computer programming languages.

Quiz

1 Who wrote the earliest known multiplication tables in around 1900 BC?

2 What branch of math is about shapes, curves, and angles?

3 What did the astronomer Ptolemy and other ancient scientists believe was at the center of the universe?

4 What was Charles Babbage's Difference Engine?

5 What was the name of the computer for which Ada Lovelace made an algorithm?

6 Why was Emmy Noether removed from her university post in Germany in 1933?

7 What household objects did the young Grace Hopper take to pieces to see how they worked?

8 What does COBOL stand for?

9 Which astronaut asked Katherine Johnson to check the computer calculations for his flight?

10 Which medal was Maryam Mirzakhani awarded in Seoul in 2014?

ANSWERS

1. The Babylonians **2.** Geometry **3.** Earth **4.** An early calculating machine **5.** The Analytical Engine **6.** Because she was Jewish **7.** Alarm clocks **8.** Common Business Oriented Language **9.** John Glenn **10.** The Fields Medal

Key Words

algorithm: a detailed step-by-step instruction or formula for solving a problem. In computing, programmers write algorithms to instruct the computer how to perform a task.

computer program: a set of instructions that tell a computer to perform an action

flight paths: the paths made, or routes taken, in air or space by spacecraft or airplanes

geometry: a branch of math that studies lines, angles, curves, surfaces, and solids

gravitational pull: a strong, irresistible force that pulls two objects toward each other

mathematical proofs: ways of showing that a mathematical idea is true and works in all places it occurs in math

momentum: strength or force gained by moving

NASA: the National Aeronautics and Space Administration, a U.S. organization responsible for space research

navigation: the act of getting a car, ship, aircraft, or spacecraft from one place to another

Nazis: members of a political party that controlled Germany from 1933 to 1945 under Adolf Hitler

orbit: one complete trip around Earth, or another body, in space

philosopher: a person who thinks deeply and seriously about the meaning of life and the universe

polymath: a person of wide knowledge, or learning

segregation: separation based on a category, such as race

theorem: a formula or prediction in math, based on reasoning

Index

LIGHTBOX

SUPPLEMENTARY RESOURCES

Click on the plus icon found in the bottom left corner of each spread to open additional teacher resources.

- Download and print the book's quizzes and activities
- Access curriculum correlations
- Explore additional web applications that enhance the Lightbox experience

LIGHTBOX DIGITAL TITLES

Packed full of integrated media

VIDEOS

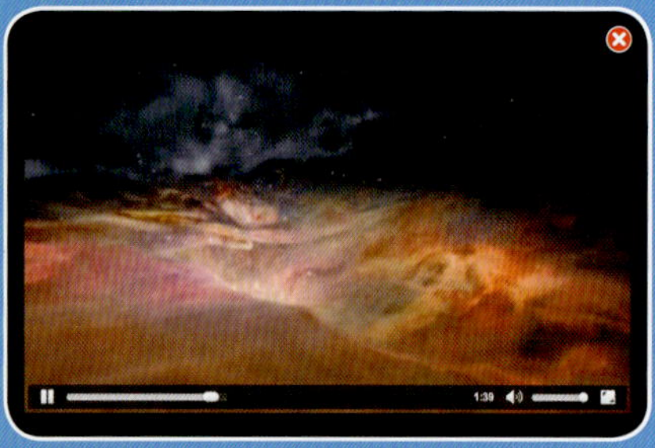

INTERACTIVE MAPS

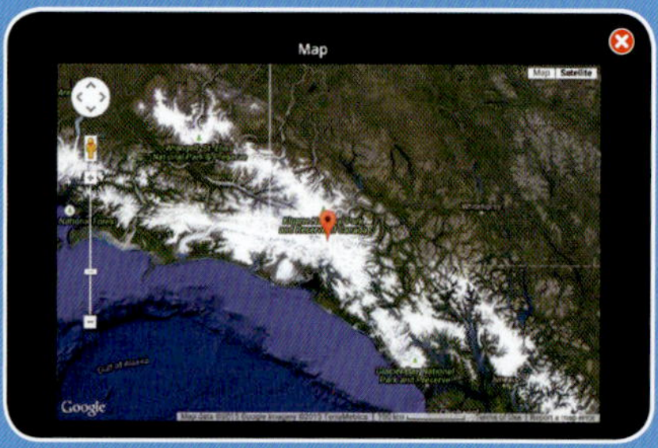

WEBLINKS

SLIDESHOWS

QUIZZES

OPTIMIZED FOR

- ✔ TABLETS
- ✔ WHITEBOARDS
- ✔ COMPUTERS
- ✔ AND MUCH MORE!

Published by Smartbook Media Inc.
350 5th Avenue, 59th Floor New York, NY 10118
Website: www.openlightbox.com

Project Coordinator: Heather Kissock
Art Director: Terry Paulhus

Library of Congress Control Number: 2019942201

ISBN 978-1-5105-4431-4 (hardcover)
ISBN 978-1-5105-4432-1 (multi-user eBook)

Printed in Guangzhou, China
1 2 3 4 5 6 7 8 9 0 23 22 21 20 19

072019
311218

Photo Credits
Every reasonable effort has been made to trace ownership and to obtain permission to reprint copyright material. The publisher would be pleased to have any errors or omissions brought to its attention so that they may be corrected in subsequent printings.

The publisher acknowledges Getty Images, Alamy, Wikimedia, Dreamstime, and Shutterstock as its primary image suppliers for this title.